Being You

A Journal for Birthmothers

Michelle Thorne

www.michellethornebooks.com

To Matthew,
with love.

Ever-present paint on your fingers

and poetry on your tongue

that causes me to come undone,

when I sat down to write this,

from my heart and for fun,

I couldn't think of one

single...thing...to say.

I had things to say to you

of passion and love and moments between us two.

They were too much for the page,

it was too big, and then, I knew

this little sentence would have to do...

Would that it were so simple.

Also by Michelle Thorne:

Delivered: My Harrowing Journey as a Birthmother

Revealing You: A Journal for Birthmothers

Mine, Yours & Ours

TABLE OF CONTENTS

Preface

Chapters

Ongoing Help

References

PREFACE

When I sat down to write *Revealing You*, it was an exercise in talking women through the first few years after placing a child for adoption. At the time I worked as a birth parent counselor for Bethany Christian Services in Little Rock, Arkansas, and helping women through those first moments, weeks, and years was a large part of what I did. I also facilitated a support group for birthmothers that was as much for me as it was for them. With the weight of my job came the need to organize the core of what I believed would help people through this massively emotional beating we call adoption.

What I didn't know then, I mean, I knew, but I didn't know, was that the emotional beating happens on every side of the triad. If I'm being honest, I didn't really want to know. I was okay with everyone feeling their feelings as long as they were overall positive. It was a fairy tale to protect my own heart. As I learned and worked in adoption during those three years in Little Rock, with the best team ever, I began to see that my fears were founded in my insecurities.

If *Revealing You* was about finding out your new normal inside of adoption, *Being You* is about accepting and living out who you are inside of it. *Being You* is born of a deep desire to talk about, process through, and survive the emotional beating that keeps happening for years to come as a birthmother.

In that respect, *Being You* is about an awareness of the multilevel plot happening inside your adoption relationship and getting you to explore it, process it, and (possibly) change your perceptions/behavior in and of it. It's a big task. It's a lot to think about, and if you are like me, you don't want to do all that work. You do, but you don't. Grief is hard. I mean, it is haaaaaard.

I wonder though, is it harder to be surprised when the grief hits you "out of nowhere" or to be practicing wholehearted living? What if we could see this thing, this part of our story on a molecular level and a global scale at the same time? How do we get to a place of functioning, celebrating and enjoying life even, after placement? Can we experience intense grief and intense joy at the same time and hold it together?

In my opinion, most of the downfall of birth parent counseling/support is that it is grief-focused. The grief is big, yes, but the joy is big too. In my experience, the birth parent experience is both/and. It doesn't give in to one or the other, it can't have one without the other. Both grief and joy. Both certainty and faith. Both informed choice and unavoidable ignorance.

If you think about a boxer stepping into the ring, you can envision part of what I think being a birthmom is like eighteen years later. I don't fight every day, but I do train for it. I accept the fight is going to hurt, I prep for how I will counter attacks. I envision positive outcomes. I know big events happen where I will have to swing hard and make contact, but I also know that muscle memory will serve me well in those times. Being a boxer is a day in and day out practice of skills that you need to be second nature when the time comes.

There is a second thing that I associate with as a birthmother, and that is being a writer. Writing, for me, is the thing I have a deep passion for that I just cannot stop being a part of. It's a love of mine. It's who I am and who I want to be at the same time. Most writers are what I call "slash writers." For example, I am a social worker/writer.

My hope is that you can move through this journal at your own pace, in your own way and begin to think of yourself as a boxer/writer, or in this case, both a practicer of wholehearted living and an engaging, child-centered-relationship participant inside of your adoption story. Navigating this was always going to be difficult, but you are worthy of love and belonging inside of this complex relationship.

1

KINTSUGI WARRIOR

You may be wondering what is on the front cover of this journal. It's a close up of a piece of pottery restored by the Japanese art of kintsugi.

In Japanese philosophy there exists the idea of "wabi-sabi," the act of embracing the flawed or the imperfect. Kintsugi in Japanese pottery is when you restore a broken piece of pottery by mending the pieces back together with lacquer that has flecks of precious metal (often gold) in it. The result is a whole piece of useful pottery with the cracks highlighted, rather than hidden. The end result of these works is beautiful.

As a birthmother, I resonate with kintsugi. For a long time, I felt unworthy of being whole, and I certainly felt undeserving of a relationship with my son. I stood on the outside, believing I shouldn't go in and at the same time, clinging to any glimpse of him I got. I didn't want him to know the real me, see my broken parts, or risk failing him. I thought he might be disappointed, feel angry at me, or worse, obligated to interact with me.

As I got healthier, I began to see how all of this was about me, my fear, and my issues. I realized that I was robbing my child of the opportunity for answers, a relationship, and love. I was looking at myself in pieces and deciding I wasn't able to be a whole anymore.

Friend, I was wrong.

Now, I like to see myself as a kintsugi warrior. I am owning my broken pieces that make me whole. I am fighting hard for love and life with my battle scars displayed across my heart and my words. The brokenness has taught me how to get back up and fight, and it's branded me as a survivor, a warrior.

You, birthmother, are a kintsugi warrior too. Your scars, the broken parts of you, are valuable. They are part of your history, part of what makes you who you are today. Yes, you are different now, but you're the same too. And you are a survivor, like me. The challenge as a birthmom is to figure out how the broken parts make you better and how they are part of your whole. Embracing the cracked pieces of your past is so important inside the adoption relationship. More importantly, you should prepare your heart to keep embracing them.

My hope for you in this journal, as you process through the pages and questions is to find self-acceptance that turns into love that creates confidence. I want you to walk away from this book knowing you are enough. I pray that you begin to hold your head high as you are, shrug off shame (because that stuff is poison), and engage within your adoption relationship with a whole heart. I want you, every day, to bring the full weight of who you are and make people deal with it.

What are the broken parts of your past? Have you let them stay broken? What do you need to restore them to a whole? Do you see yourself as whole? Can you begin to see the grief and suffering you've experienced as valuable? What has it taught you? How have these lessons shaped who you are or changed your relationships?

How do you see yourself? When you mess up, is your self-talk positive or negative? Who taught you how to talk this way to yourself? What do you like about yourself? What do you like about your body? What do you like about your personality? How does your image of yourself need to change? What lies do you believe that you need to speak truth into? What practical steps can you take to love yourself well? What can you do or say daily to transform your mind to the truth of how worthy you are of love and belonging?

BE YOU to full, *Beautiful!*

BE YOU to full, *Beautiful!*

BE YOU to full, *Beautiful!*

BE YOU to full, *Beautiful!*

BE YOU to full, Beautiful!

BE YOU to full, *Beautiful!*

BE YOU to full, *Beautiful!*

BE YOU to full, *Beautiful!*

2

KEEPING THE CHILD AT THE CENTER

Adoption is both concrete and ethereal. For adoptive parents, it's ethereal and then concrete. They have a dream, and then they are chosen to parent a child. For adoptees, it's both ethereal and concrete for the span of their lives. They are adopted, and they don't know their whole story. For birth parents, it's concrete first. There is a child. He is yours. You physically place him. Then, it gets ethereal. What is he doing today? When did he take his first steps? When he cried in the night was anyone there to comfort him. Does he know I love him?

When I got away from the 'event' (the day I placed my son for adoption), I was relieved at first. *I made it. I did it. He will be well and well loved.* It was a story I told myself and prayed it would be true because if it wasn't, what had I just done?

Over time, that relief turned into a million questions. The search for where I fit in inside my adoption story led me to Jesus, which led me to self-discovery and that let me to Brené Brown. Throughout this process, I was working in adoption in different capacities. I began to tell my story a lot, hear from adoptees, care for adoptees and their families, and have honest conversations with adoptive parents both pre and post placement.

I learned a lot. I learned that I was both complicit and not solely at fault for not maintaining contact. I didn't think I was worthy of a relationship with him and neither did anyone else at the time. When I placed my son, adoption professionals were not pushing open adoption relationships, but they recommended some contact in the beginning and then nothing after five years. (I'm glad we know better now, but that doesn't help how I lived the first ten years of his life.)

I learned that the less contact I had, the more I questioned my decision to place him. I realized that my lack of contact was founded in my insecurities. I became educated about child development, and I learned that my reasons for a lack of contact were about me, not him. What began with an intrinsic motivation to love my son well, had dwindled into a lack of follow through on my part in contact, opportunity, and connection.

Learning that, taught me this: If we all work to keep the child at the center of the relationship consistently, we will maintain healthy adoption relationships. This means having child-centered goals and boundaries. This demands forgiving and asking for forgiveness. This sets up parents (birth and adoptive) for hurt because none of them are at the center and by nature, that can/will hurt at some point. However, would you rather be hurt or your child be hurt?

Think about it.

Why did you place your child for adoption? What obstacles kept you from parenting? Who was encouraging you? Who was discouraging you? How did you feel about others opinions about your pregnancy/placing?

With those things sorted out.

How do you feel now that you have gotten away from the 'event'? Do you still feel that adoption was the right choice for you? What more do you want to learn about adoption or your child? How, if at all, would you change your adoption relationship?

Are there parts of your adoption story that are yet to be redeemed? Do you need to forgive someone? Do you need to forgive yourself?

If you are to keep your adoption relationship child-centered, how can you work to focus on your child throughout difficult interactions/exchanges/ life stages? If your child doesn't want to see you right now or in the future, how are/will you handle that? What positive coping mechanisms do you have in place for rejection? What can you do in the absence of contact with your child that still convey your love for him/her?

If you and your child's adoptive parents can come into the relationship at each point of contact with the child at the center and the child's best interest at heart, you have a shot at a long, healthy adoption relationship. You get to choose pre and post placement to love and keep loving big. When in doubt, friends, think of your child's best interest and choose love.

BE YOU to full, *Beautiful!*

BE YOU to full, *Beautiful!*

BE YOU to full, *Beautiful!*

BE YOU to full, *Beautiful!*

BE YOU to full, *Beautiful!*

BE YOU to full, Beautiful!

BE YOU to full, *Beautiful!*

BE YOU to full, *Beautiful!*

3

THE TWO LOVES

Remember when you first learned about your child's parents? If you chose them, you liked them for some reason, right? What were those reasons? Were they kind-hearted or educated? Did they love others well? What about them made you feel like you could trust them as your child's parents (if you chose them)? If you didn't choose, are there things you like about them? Do you have things in common with them?

It's important to remember the beginning because relationships change because people change. Our perspectives shift over time, and when we look back, we might see things differently or realize a new thing. That can be good and bad.

Perspective is important, and the fact that it changes is important. Let's take love for example. When you chose to place your child, love was involved on some level. People talk about love, using the same word and meaning two completely different things.

You may tell me that you have a love that has four sides, and I might reply that mine does too. You may let me know your love has four corners that are all right angles, and I would agree because so does mine. But when you hold up a picture of what your love looks like and I hold up a picture of what my love looks like, yours is a square and mine is a rectangle. If we were toddlers with a shapes toy, your love wouldn't fit into my love and vice versa.

This is so important because we need to expect it inside our adoption relationships. Love can be just as fierce, just as true, and look different. Not better, not worse, just different. The exciting thing with these relationships is that there is room inside the child for all this love. Not only will your love most certainly, at least to some degree, look different from the parents you chose to place your child with, but your love will look different from what your child's love looks like too.

So, what? We all just run around loving in our own way? Yes, and no. We pay attention. You can love your child the best you know how at any given moment. So, as you change and grow and as your child changes and grows, your love can look different. And you pay attention to how your child loves and receives love. You pay attention to how your child's adoptive parents love, and though it is different from yours, you can celebrate their efforts (and they yours!).

I love this idea because it gives me as a birthmom freedom. I get to choose how to love my child. I don't have to make physical contact, like I will talk about later in this journal, to love my child well at any given moment. I love him when I choose to pray for him or donate money to his school or forgive myself for placing him for adoption instead of wallowing in the self-pity associated with it.

Love is a big, complex idea. It's physical and emotional, and it looks different for everyone. C.S. Lewis famously wrote, "Love is not affectionate feeling, but a steady wish for the loved person's ultimate good as far as it can be obtained." If we are loving our children like that, then there is room for all the shapes that love comes in.

How have you loved your child well? In what non-contact ways do you choose to love your child? What are some new ways you want to love your child well? How have you seen your child's adoptive parents loving your child in a way that you didn't anticipate? What ways do they love your child that looks different from what you do? Is there a way you can complement what they do? Is there a way that you would like to see them compliment what you do?

BE YOU to full, *Beautiful!*

BE YOU to full, Beautiful!

BE YOU to full, *Beautiful!*

BE YOU to full, *Beautiful!*

BE YOU to full, *Beautiful!*

BE YOU to full, *Beautiful!*

BE YOU to full, *Beautiful*!!

4

FITTING IN VS. BELONGING

Do you ever struggle inside of your adoption relationship, trying to figure out your place? I mean, we birthmoms aren't exactly on the outside, right? The child wouldn't be here without us choosing life, carrying that child to term, facing all the emotions in the world on the day our child is born, and living each day afterward. But we aren't exactly on the inside either. We don't know the daily ins and outs of our child's life. We miss the first steps, the first words, being called 'mom,' holding them when they are sick and needy, and everything in between. So, where does that leave us?

In my experience, most of us timidly walk the perimeter of our child's life. We hold onto any information we get with a death grip. We are (usually) only fed happy stories, giving us an unrealistic view of what's going on in our child's life and shocking us when they grow up and reveal anything painful. It's weird. If I'm strong enough to handle placing a child for adoption, aren't I strong enough to hear that my child was bullied at school or has been diagnosed with an illness or disease? And if I'm given this privileged information, where do I go with it? Am I close enough to touch that subject? Am I allowed to feel differently about it than others do? How do I handle these things when I'm his mom but not his mom?

In her book *The Gifts of Imperfection* (Hazelden, 2010), Brené Brown writes, "Fitting in is about assessing a situation and becoming who you need to be to be accepted. Belonging, on the other hand, doesn't require us to change who we are; it requires us to be who we are." I have rarely seen this in adoption. Most often, all three entities are looking to fit in with each other. So often we birth parents are so thrilled at the opportunity to connect with our child that we will stretch our beliefs, not speak up when we think we should, and/or hide information, feelings, hopes, etcetera to fit in. But if we are fitting in, and fitting in is counter to belonging, are we not robbing ourselves of a deeper, better relationship with one that we love?

This truth was a game changer for me in my adoption relationship. I had spent a lot of time trying to figure out what was best for everyone else and attempting to interpret how others would react to my every move. I wanted it to be so perfect that I didn't make any moves for a long time. I worked hard to assess a situation I couldn't accurately evaluate and therefore, robbed myself of the opportunity for connection. If we are going to belong inside our adoption relationships, and I think we do and should, we are going to have to risk failure and freely offer forgiveness to ourselves and others when failures happen.

Belonging requires that we know ourselves. We need to get comfortable in our own skin and inside our own story to be able to offer who we are to another person. If we want the deep connection we desire to come to fruition, we are going to have to show up inside this relationship and be seen as we truly are. Belonging is the daily practice of choosing to be yourself.

So, the next time you are struggling with where your place is inside the adoption relationship, where your connection is and isn't, and where you belong, instead of trying to figure out what is expected of you or what others think you should do, just be yourself. Press into the complexity and uncertainty of the adoption relationship. Consider being vulnerable. Saying things like, 'I don't know,' 'I'm afraid,' and 'I'm sorry' are all valid, relatable, and essential for you and the others inside the relationship.

What does it look like when you are yourself? What are things you say and do when you are comfortable with yourself? What do you hide when you are trying to fit in? Who can you practice being yourself with? Who is a person you feel like you belong with? How are your actions with those you belong to different from those you try to fit in with? How do you feel when you belong compared to when you fit in?

Have you ever tried to simply fit in with your child or adoptive parents? How did the interaction go? Were you satisfied with the level of connection? What would being seen look like for you? What emotions or feelings would be revealed if you were to be yourself during an interaction with your child and/or his parents?

BE YOU to full, Beautiful!

BE YOU to full, *Beautiful!*

BE YOU to full, Beautiful!

BE YOU to full, Beautiful!

BE YOU to full, Beautiful!

BE YOU to full, *Beautiful!*

BE YOU to full, *Beautiful!*

BE YOU to full, *Beautiful!*

5

INDEPENDENTLY CONNECTED

One of the best and hardest lessons I have ever learned (and have to be re-taught) is that I can only control myself. At any given moment, no matter who I am responsible for or who I am in a relationship with, I cannot control any person apart from myself. Think of it this way: If you draw a circle around yourself, you can control everyone inside your circle.

Is your child inside your circle? No.
Is your child's family, parents, grandparents, siblings inside your circle? No.
Is your husband or any other children you may have inside your circle? No.
You alone are inside your circle. You by yourself, as you are. That's it. You are the only person you can control.

I have struggled with this because I want to get into people's circle and make them do what I want or what I think is right. Some people like others to come into their circle and pass blame. The cold, hard truth is that you can only control yourself, and that is especially relevant inside of an adoption relationship.

We are all—birth parents, adoptive parents and adoptees—independently connected to each other. What I mean by that is we are each responsible for our part of the relationship, and we cannot force another to do more than he/she is willing to do, nor should we try. If years of adoption research and the call for adoption reform has taught us anything, it's that the voice of the adoptee is the most valuable voice in the adoption relationship. We need to listen and respond, but we should not force, manipulate or control.

As an adoption professional, I have seen a wide variety of situations, some of them negative. Birth parents who are not interacting with their children because of their own insecurities (I was guilty of this.) or refusing to have a relationship with adoptive parents because of jealousy or unresolved anger and resentment. I have seen adoptive parents opt out of the relationship out of fear or poor adoption education. I have also known adoptees who wanted more from their birth parents and those who wanted nothing. However, if we look around inside our circle, we can see who and what we can control, and we can connect on our own, the best we can. We don't have to rely on the other party to be connected. We can, right now, no matter how in touch we are, be connected to our child and his family. We can do something.

If your child doesn't want contact, you can continue to write cards and catalog your life. If your child's parents have chosen to step away, no matter the reason, you can still buy gifts and pen letters. You can tell a story by how you connect and what you choose to do with what you can control.

If you have no connection with your child or his family now, you can still do something, and why would you want to? Because you love your child and with your child's best interest in mind, you know that connection is vital for both of you. People change. Circumstances change. Hopefully, there will be a day when you can share all these things you have used to create connection in your child's "absence" and then, how do you think they will feel when they see your efforts over all these years?

If you have an ongoing connection, you still can only control yourself. Think through what you want your relationship to look like. Know that your relationship will change as your child grows. Consider that your child's parents are not parenting experts, but people who also love your child and will sometimes get it wrong. Practice gratitude and forgiveness with and for your child and his parents. Sometimes you are going to be the one teaching them how to do this relationship well.

As your child grows, remember to keep them at the center of the relationship. Ask them to share their stories with you. Ask them to teach you about themselves. Consider asking them permission to share on social media before doing it. If there comes a time when your child needs some space, remember they are not inside your circle, but they are at the center of this relationship. Work hard to give them the freedom they need, whether it is a close relationship or a more distant one, and remember that change is sure to come.

In any type of adoption relationship, consider that others do not know or understand your perspective. Share, educate and advocate for yourself. Know that you are the only one who can help them understand what you might want or feel at any given moment, and don't be afraid to ask them what they want and feel too. Be brave, friends.

Who have you let inside your circle? What do you need to do to get them out of it? Who are you trying to bring into your circle to control? Who are you blaming for things that are your responsibility? Who do you need to stand up to for your circle to be secure? How have your child's adoptive parents loved you or disappointed you? How can you practice gratitude inside of your adoption relationship? How can you practice forgiveness inside your adoption relationship? What do you need to do to remember that you can only control yourself?

BE YOU to full, *Beautiful!*

BE YOU to full, *Beautiful!*

BE YOU to full, *Beautiful!*

BE YOU to full, *Beautiful!*

BE YOU to full, *Beautiful!*

BE YOU to full, *Beautiful!*

BE YOU to full, *Beautiful!*

6

OPEN-HEARTED CONFLICT

Relationships are hard work. They take time, attention, and sacrifice. Relationships are also built on trust. You need to know inside your close relationships that the other person will do what they say and care for your heart in a way that is safe, aside from the slip up here or there. On a core level, you have to know that you trust this person.

I think when we place our children with a person or a couple, we initially trust them. Even if we don't say the words, we hand them the most precious thing in our lives and say, 'Take care of him/her.' There is an attitude of trust, a posture of openness. We hope and believe on some level that this person is worthy of taking care of our child.

I'm not going to ask you to think about when these people will screw it up, because we know they will, on some level at some time. In adoption, disappointment is inevitable. What I want you to think about is yourself. When you have moments where you don't feel like these people are trustworthy anymore, or in this one circumstance, and you wonder what happened, how do you respond? If you haven't experienced this, be thankful, but know that you need to prepare your heart.

Conflict is like failure, it gets a bad rap. I love conflict, in a way. I grew up hating it, but I see the value in it now. Yes, it's uncomfortable, but it creates opportunities for connection too. People respond to conflict in different ways. I shut down, think about what I want to say/do, and then speak up or do what I need to. Some people attack. Some people-please. Some run.

Think through conflicts in your life. What is your typical response to conflict? Did your response create connection or disconnection? Does your response depend on the other person?

That last one is a crucial question. Does your response to conflicts depend on the other person in the conflict? Because, friend, it shouldn't. If you make your responses in conflict or connection based on the other person, you are saying to them, "You have the power." You are essentially, letting them into your circle and saying, you are in charge here.

No. Just no.

When conflicts arise, we want to make our own choices because we are the only ones living with those choices. Think about when you placed (i.e. a significant conflict). Who encouraged you to place? Are they living with the daily struggle of birth parenting? Do they go through the grief? Probably not.

On a much smaller scale, when your child's adoptive parents don't send you those pictures on time or when they put him in public school when they said they were going to put him in a private school like you wanted (or whatever else), you are going to be the one living with your choice to speak up for yourself, shut down and say nothing, lie and tell them it's fine, or attack them. And because you are going to be the one living with the consequences , you have to respond based on you, your needs, you're wishes. It may not turn out like you want, but still, I implore you, make your response one you can live with.

What conflicts have you had with your child or the adoptive parents? How did you respond in those conflicts? Did you feel more connected or disconnected afterward? Did you feel like you had to go along with whatever they wanted to keep a connection with your child? Did you regret your response in any way? Are you comfortable agreeing to disagree with your child/child's adoptive parents?

Now, let's go back to the building block of this relationship. It was trust, on some level. Even if they have blown that out of the water in your opinion, it started there. If you can attempt to maintain a posture of openness and trust with these people, conflicts will be more manageable. When conflict arises, instead of making assumptions or acting out of fear, if you can try to plug yourself into the trust that the relationship was built on, you may react differently.

When there is conflict in a trusting relationship, people own their part of the conflict.

I was wrong when I did that. I'm sorry I said this.

When there is conflict in a trusting relationship, people respond with open-ended questions.

Can you tell me why? Can you help me understand?

When there is conflict in a trusting relationship, people say "I" statements.

When you did this, I felt like that. I don't understand this. I want to know more.

When there is conflict in a trusting relationship, people don't assume the worst. They don't assume that the conflict is solely about them. They don't assume the other party knows what they want. These adoptive parents have never been birth parents (likely), and so they have no idea of the experience you are having. They don't know how hard a late update is or a long lag of silence. They don't understand why Mother's Day sucks, no matter what they do. Don't be afraid to help them.

Do you have unresolved conflict in your adoption relationship? Have you owned your part of the conflicts? Have you made any assumptions that you would like to clear up? What are some open-ended questions you need to ask right now? What "I" statements do you need to practice? How can you keep your child at the center of your adoption relationship when conflict occurs? How can you prepare your heart for conflict inside your adoption relationship?

Here are some basic tips for conflict:
- Own your part of the conflict.
- Know when to let it go and when to address it, seeking wise counsel if you are unsure.
- Name the offense without bringing up other things.
- Ask open-ended questions and use "I" statements.
- Never assume the other person knows what you think, want, or need.
- Forgiveness (of yourself and others) is essential for relationships to move forward in love.

If you need further help with conflict, I highly recommend *Resolving Everyday Conflict* by Ken Sande and Kevin Johnson (Baker Books, 2015).

BE YOU to full, *Beautiful!*

BE YOU to full, *Beautiful!*

BE YOU to full, Beautiful!

BE YOU to full, *Beautiful!*

BE YOU to full, *Beautiful!*

BE YOU to full, Beautiful!

7

TRANSFORMING FAILURE

Failure.

It's such a dirty word with so much baggage. Worse than that, it is so relatable. Everyone in the world can relate to failure, and failure is so negative. It's a nasty little bugger that we want nothing to do with. Problem is, it's vital to our lives.

You are going to fail at something, at some point, and definitely inside of your adoption relationship. It is inevitable. Don't despise it. Instead, get prepared for it, so when it comes, you know how to deal with it.

If you think about it, all failure is, is transformation. It's the moment of change, of realization. It's the time when we wake up and go, "Oh, that didn't work." Outside of all of our emotions and physical striving, it's just that simple. Failure has a lot of emotional, physical, social, financial, etc. things attached to it, but boiled down it's just something different from what we originally thought. It's new information that shifts our perspective, thoughts, and choices in the future.

Notice I didn't say it's the opposite of success. I truly believe that success can look like failure. Take the death of Jesus, for example.

So, transformation and failure as a success...Yes, I think we need to change our idea about failure. What if we looked at failures as successes to transform into something better? If caterpillars and math equations can do it without it being negative, maybe we can too.

What does that mean though, in view of an adoption relationship? Well, let's think about it this way. If you want to belong, so you choose to be yourself with your different-looking love, and you get in there and bring the full weight of who you are and make them deal with it, but then, disaster strikes and you fail in some way, at some point, what happens then?

If you are practicing replacing the negativity and baggage of failure with the positivity and promise of transformation, you will be free to change. If you recognize that you failed your child or your child's adoptive parents, you can stop, ask forgiveness, and move onto the change. You can involve them in the transition. *"What can I do better next time?"* You can spend more time on the connection in the relationship instead of obsessing about the disconnection you created.

Always remember to keep your child at the center of your relationship with the adoptive parents. Who will benefit from you slinking away into oblivion after a failure? No one. Your child deserves your best fight to get back in there and try again. Don't allow anyone to explain your struggles to your child. When you fall down, get back up and try again.

What if it's been a long time, you wonder? I would say stand up and fight. Fight for your relationship with your child. Sometimes the grief of the birthmom train derails us, sometimes for years. Friend, do not be ashamed. You are not alone. Reach out to someone who can hear you and help you stand strong.

What are some things that have made you feel like a failure inside your adoption relationship? Have any of your failures made you change for the better? What failures have left you feeling distanced from your child/child's adoptive parents? How can you engage in your adoption relationship in new ways where you have struggled in the past? What would a transformation look like inside of you as part of your adoption relationship? How can you keep your child at the center of the relationship when you make mistakes? Who will benefit from you choosing to rise strongly when you fail?

BE YOU to full, *Beautiful!*

BE YOU to full, Beautiful!

BE YOU to full, *Beautiful!*

BE YOU to full, *Beautiful!*

BE YOU to full, *Beautiful!*

BE YOU to full, *Beautiful!*

BE YOU to full, *Beautiful!*

BE YOU to full, *Beautiful!*

BE YOU to full, *Beautiful!*

8

DIGITAL FOOTPRINTS

When thinking through writing this book, one of the driving forces behind it was the digital age. We are a bunch of selfie-obsessed, digital junkies. We love to see who's doing what, when, where and why. We put ourselves (not our true selves, mind you) out there for the world to see. Why do we do this? In a word, *connection*. We are built for community and relationship.

That can be good news! We are inside an adoption relationship. We were built for connection. Surely this thing will go smoothly, right? Wrong. People are people.

When you think about your digital footprint, think of it as concrete, not sand. Whatever you are putting out there on the internet, no matter the intention can be perverted and transformed. Trust me. I'm a closet graphic designer, I know these things. I just transformed a .gif of Noah Centineo to make it look like he was kissing a friend of mine for her birthday. Yeah, I know. I'm a good friend, but I digress. Anything you put on the internet can be changed, if only by a misconception inside someone's mind.

This is especially true of words. When we teach children about gossip, we take a tube of toothpaste, empty it out and ask them to put it all back in. They can't. Neither can you. You may be thinking, I'm not gossiping about my child, but are you over-sharing? Your words have power, spoken and/or written, and written words lose the context of facial expressions and voice inflection.

Take, for example, this text exchange yesterday between my husband and me. I had been annoyed that morning because, well, it was morning and I was responsible for people getting to school when, well, it was morning. Need I say more??? Anyway, at five in the evening:

Him-"In the cab (on the way home). You?"
Me-"Fine."

Him-"F.I.N.E."
Me-"What-ever."

My phone rang immediately.
"Hello?" I asked.
"What's wrong?"
"Nothing," I said.
My husband paused. "Oh, I thought you were upset."
I laughed. "And I thought you were being funny so I was too."

It happens so easily with the best intentions. We live in a day and age when people are being vetted digitally before getting jobs. The world is watching our stories unfold before them as we share the good, the bad, and the ugly publicly to strangers. We are letting others decide who we are and what we stand for based on our social status and that is not necessarily a great thing.

What does that mean for you inside of your adoption relationship? Have you ever heard the saying, "That's my story and I'm sticking to it?" What if your story wasn't told by you? Did you ever have your parents tell an embarrassing story about you to someone you didn't want to know that particular story? How did that work out? Sometimes, it helps a person know you and helps you understand how they will, or will not, accept the real you. Sometimes, it backfires. When we put our children out on social media, we tell their story. Some of it is harmless, but there may be things that they will grow up and not want out there for the world to see. Remember that your child has a digital footprint that will last his whole life. Consider asking your child's (parents', if they are too young) permission before sharing pictures or personal stories on social media.

There is also the matter of just plain privacy. When we invite everyone we know on social media, and let's face it some of them we don't know, we are inviting them into our child's life. We may not want everyone to know our child's information, image, successes, or failures. Why? Because the world is small.

What happens when your child starts a school and his teacher knows more about his story than you do because he or she knows your child's adoptive parents well? How would you feel if your child was asked hard questions about his life/story/you on the playground because all of his information was out there for the world to know? What if your child is working through his identity and/or adoption story and other adults are offering him information instead of the trusted people in his life because it's out there on social media? How would you feel if someone you know, God forbid someone who doesn't like you, contacts your child or his parents and tells them everything about you that you may not be ready to share with them yet? What if your child finds out you are getting married or are pregnant again before you have a chance to tell them?

Social media can be a useful tool for connection, but it can be crippling too. I'm not an advocate of secrecy, but I do believe in privacy. Everyone online has not earned the right to hear or be in your story, or your child's story. Think through what you are sharing, why you are sharing it, and who it's about. If you are posting about you, fine. If you are giving away your child's story, don't. Think of your child and what you want his life to look like in twenty years. Let him decide what gets shared about him and what doesn't. These stories, like our children, are sacred. They are spaces not meant for everyone. Choose who, what, when, and how you share your children with people you love. Your child is worth holding close to your heart.

Who has earned the right to hear your whole story? Who can you trust with the intimate details of your life? What stories do you love to share most about your child? Are any of the parts shared not about you or your story? How would you feel if you heard someone else tell your story? What are you willing for others to know who are not as connected to you? How can you protect your child's privacy and still talk about your adoption relationship? What outlets (Snapchat, Facebook, Instagram, word of mouth, etc.) have you agreed to use/not use when talking about your child? What are the advantages of sharing your story? What are the disadvantages of sharing your story?

BE YOU to full, *Beautiful!*

BE YOU to full, *Beautiful!*

BE YOU to full, *Beautiful!*

BE YOU to full, *Beautiful!*

BE YOU to full, *Beautiful!*

BE YOU to full, *Beautiful!*

BE YOU to full, *Beautiful!*

BE YOU to full, *Beautiful!*

9

LOVE RELATIONSHIPS

After I placed my son for adoption, I believed, and often said, 'No man will ever love me, especially if they love God.' It was something that caused me to go on dates flippantly. I knew I wasn't worthy of love and so who cared, right? Wrong.

When I met my husband, he changed my mind and my life—not because he swooped in and rescued my broken self, but because he vulnerably revealed to me his broken self. He didn't need me to be perfect, and he valued my heart, the parts that were whole and thriving and the parts that ached and needed mending. It was stunning and beautiful. Without saying the words, he told me I was worthy of love.

Friend, you are too.

After placement, as life moves and takes on a regular pace, you may begin to think about dating. If you weren't married when you placed, or you were married and are no longer, dating may re-enter the picture.

Once you place and have some time and space between you and the 'event,' which you know by now adoption is a lifelong journey and not an event, your life will take on a new normal. Part of that new normal may be a new love relationship. Before you placed, you could just go out on a date and have fun. Now, these people are being held to higher standards. You can't just say yes to anyone. Your idea of fun may be different. Now, well, there is so much more to consider.

How would this person respond to the information that you are a birthmother?
What are this person's opinions of adoption?
Would you want this person interacting with your child?
Will this person respect your boundaries and wishes with sex, privacy, and grief?

Will this person fully accept your child as yours inside of the complex adoption relationship?

Prior to dating anyone, you may consider thinking through the outcomes of these and other questions about your adoption relationship. Think through the ending. Love yourself and your child enough to stop and consider your 'ultimate good as far as it can be obtained,' to quote C.S. Lewis again. Know that you are worth loving, as you choose who you will date.

When you do begin to get serious, there's even more to consider. Marriage often means children will follow.

Will this person support your relationship with your child as life changes?
Will this person support the sibling connection your children with have with the child you placed?
Is this person safe for your grief, when he may be ecstatic over your new addition(s)?
Could you talk openly and honestly about your adoption relationship with your spouse and would you be able to with your future children?
How does this person's family feel about your adoption relationship?

Marriage, like adoption, is not an event but a lifelong journey. And if you don't know this already, I've been married fourteen years at the time I am writing this and let me tell you, it is hard. H.A.R.D. Doing life with another person is just that—doing life. And we all know that life is hard.

When you begin to think about dating again or marriage after placement, another thing to consider is space. You need to prepare your heart to allow this other person to have some space. Know that just like people grieve in different ways, they receive and process information in different ways. When you talk about your adoption relationship, know that both of you will need your own time and space to process these things, and that's okay. I'm not saying you can't do that together in different ways, but I am saying that you might not want to be together when you do it, and that's okay.

Ask yourself:

Am I able to talk about this honestly without worrying about what my partner is thinking?
Will I be upset if my partner says the 'wrong' thing?
Is my partner my solution to this problem?

Can I voice my needs (i.e., I just need you to listen, or I need you to respond objectively.) regarding this situation?
Do I need to talk with someone professional or another birthmother?

Our partners in our love relationships will not always get it right, and neither will we. At times, my husband has mishandled the situation because I didn't help him understand what I needed or I simply wanted him to make it better, which he will never be able to do. Figure out what works best for you and bring that into your love relationships. Know that you and your partner will mess this up, and practice forgiveness.

BE YOU to full, *Beautiful!*

BE YOU to full, *Beautiful!*

BE YOU to full, *Beautiful!*

BE YOU to full, *Beautiful!*

BE YOU to full, *Beautiful!*

BE YOU to full, *Beautiful!*

BE YOU to full, *Beautiful!*

10

PREGNANCY AFTER PLACEMENT

I had my heart broken last week. A friend of mine, a birthmom, messaged me on facebook (she can't call because I live in China) and said this:

Hey! So people keep asking me if this is my first baby and I keep saying yes...is that a lie? Or wrong?

Ugh. Yes. No. I don't know. None of their business.

When you are pregnant again after you have placed a child for adoption, things can get tricky. People ask you a million questions...

Is this your first baby?
Where will you have the baby?
When are you due?
How do your other children feel about this new addition?
Are you ready to be a mom?
Isn't there a lot of salt in that pickle?

...and give you a ton of advice...

Just wait until you hold that little baby, and it will all be better.
Do/Don't get the epidural.
Your body will completely change.
Pack your hospital bag early.
Do/Don't find out the sex of your child.
Register here but not there.
Get this type of stroller.
Do/Don't exclusively breastfeed

...and say stupid things...

Wide load coming through.
You're big for how long you have left in this pregnancy.
I would not want to be you.
You get to have your own baby now.
God is redeeming your story.
At least you got pregnant again.

And while most of these seem innocent enough, they bring back up the last pregnancy, the one that resulted in adoption, the one where you didn't get to bring your baby home, the one where you left the hospital empty handed and brokenhearted. This can be devastating, and it's something that no one prepared me for. I thought having that next baby would be healing. It wasn't. It didn't even touch the surface of what was going on inside me emotionally.

Everything was different. I was married. This child was planned, hoped for and celebrated by all. I received my first Mother's Day card from my mom and sisters (while I was pregnant), even though I had been celebrating Mother's Day since 2000 and it was 2008. I was thrown a baby shower. People started talking to me (positively) about God concerning pregnancy, as opposed to His judgment/disappointment.

At some point early on, I realized I was a complete mess. I had a lot of hurt, which looked like anger. Why wasn't my first child celebrated by these people? Why wasn't I more responsible in my sex life? Why did it still have to hurt so deeply?

I had a lot of guilt. I felt bad for being happy, and I felt bad for being sad. I couldn't fit myself into rejoicing when everything reminded me of my previous pregnancy, which held so much heartache. I didn't know how to talk about what I was feeling, and others didn't really want to hear it.

There is a big misconception that one will replace/heal/redeem the other. People seemed uncomfortable with my pain and wanted me just to move forward, which to them meant forgetting about the past. It just doesn't happen. Being a birthmother is not like forgiving. You don't make a choice and then forget about it. It's like shame, the soul's swampland that you wade in for the rest of your life.

If you are, have, or plan to get pregnant again after placement, get ready for some big, contrasting feelings. Prepare yourself for tears that mean two things as they fall down your face. Get ready to exercise your boundaries, say hard things to your partner, and feel all of your feelings. This one is going to hurt both like and different from the last one. Most importantly, know deep down in your soul that both of these children are yours, which makes both sets of feelings and experiences valid and wholly yours to have and to hold.

How do/did you feel about being pregnant after placement? Are/Were there things you shut out to feel the positive emotions only? How will/did you deal with the juxtaposition of feelings about being pregnant again? What are some true things about both pregnancies? What things are different? What experiences/emotions need to be validated? How can you give yourself the gift of acceptance inside your 'next' pregnancy story? How can you prepare yourself for the questions you will receive? How can you exercise proper boundaries with those you love? Who can you go to when you need to say hard things? What scares you about being pregnant again?

BE YOU to full, *Beautiful!*

BE YOU to full, *Beautiful!*

BE YOU to full, *Beautiful!*

BE YOU to full, *Beautiful!*

BE YOU to full, *Beautiful!*

BE YOU to full, *Beautiful!*

BE YOU to full, *Beautiful!*

11

PARENTING AFTER PLACEMENT

When I sat down to write this chapter, nothing came close to this blog I wrote several years ago. I've shared it before, but I have to do it again:

Today was the day that my daughter started Kindergarten. It was a big day for both of us. I walked her in the pouring rain to her school and down the hall. Tomorrow I will not get to go to her classroom. She is a big girl now. But today, I got to go.

Hand-in-hand, we walked and I looked at her. I am so fond of her. She is light and salt and a blessing. She looked back at me and gave a hint of a smile. She was excited!

In these innocent moments, these milestones, I often have company—birthmother grief. It's unforgiving and quick, like the thud of a punch on my cheek. She found her name and sat in her chair. I got down on her level and looked her in the eyes. Then, kneeling there beside my sweet daughter, I lost it.

I kissed her goodbye. I walked out of the classroom and went to my car with tears falling as freely as the rain. I felt a shadow. I felt like an elephant was sitting on my chest. I felt a sense of guilt; this was my daughter's big day. I felt tired. I have been running this race a long time.

Last year I took a job as a Pregnancy Counselor, and this job has put my personal story front and center. I see women everyday walking through different parts of a narrative I have lived. While I am honored to be a small part of their story, it still surprises me how true my Pregnancy Counselor advice is for myself.

I have waxed poetically about resurfacing grief. Last month at Imprint, the post-placement support group that I facilitate, I talked about it like it was for the other birthmothers in the room. But God knew it was for me.

"Grief comes up at life events. It doesn't get easier; you begin to recognize it. When it comes up, take a good look at it, hold it, allow yourself to feel it, and give yourself grace."

This morning, I grieved missing the joy of taking Dylan to his first day of school. I felt the distance between us, between parenting and birth parenting.

It's not just the milestones I miss, but the moments too. The excitement in his eyes as he learns. The thrill of running on the playground. The stories from school about his day. The little moments, where he smiles and waves goodbye to his mom.

His mom who takes him to school, not me. And I love her and I love her for it. I love her for all of it. For providing for him and for catching the moments and for treasuring him. I am thankful.

Still, on days like today, I can't help but feel the pull in a million different directions, like my heart is a preschool parachute.

Grief comes at life events. It doesn't get easier, you begin to recognize it.

I recognize it.

I know what this is, I think. I take a deep breath. I begin to drive, and I give in to it. I proceed to bawl my eyes out the whole way to work.

And as I park my car, I remember playing with a parachute in Mrs. Diven's P.E. class. I remember the way the parachute works. Pulled from every direction so tight it might split in two, we would hold on and yank that thing in a million directions. Everyone got to play. Everyone was needed to participate and make the parachute work.

It was a group effort.

And I wonder then, about my heart. I feel it being pulled. I feel the danger of it splitting in two. Joy for Cadence. Sadness over Dylan. Pride in my children. Grief over my children. The sweet gains. The significant losses. The hopes, the anticipations, the hurts, and the fears. My heart feels them all.

And I wonder about God. Jesus was a man well-aquatinted with grief and the Savior. He was moved with compassion and had righteous anger in the Temple. He commanded demons and He wept.

And I wonder about that preschool parachute. How it only works with a group of individuals working together all around the edges. How pulling it taut allows it to work properly. How each person attached to the parachute is necessary.

And then I recognize it. This pain reminds me that placing my son for adoption was the most loving, hardest thing I have ever done—still, to this day. I welcome the reminder. I take a good look at it, hold it, allow myself to feel it, and give myself grace.

This pain is important. This pain is connected to all the other things that I feel.

This pain lets me know I still love him this much.

When have you felt the distance between parenting and birth parenting? Did you recognize it right away or did it take some time? How did you process through your feelings? How do you allow for all the different feelings surrounding your adoption relationship? Do you talk with your child/child's parents about the pull between contrasting feelings? What life events have happened to you that made you aware of your deep pain and love for your child? Is there a life event coming that might bring up some grief and loss? How can you prepare your heart to process through the grief and loss that will surely come up again?

BE YOU to full, *Beautiful!*

BE YOU to full, *Beautiful!*

BE YOU to full, *Beautiful!*

BE YOU to full, *Beautiful!*

BE YOU to full, *Beautiful!*

BE YOU to full, *Beautiful!*

12

THE SIBLING CONNECTION

When I talk with parents about adoption, I tell them to speak with their child about adoption like they do sex—age-appropriate information from an early age. Kids have questions. They want to know where they come from. If you are like me, you may have wanted (mandated?) that your child know he was adopted from the beginning. I felt like it was crucial for his growth and search for his identity to know he was adopted, but I never considered my other children. At the time I didn't have any, and after the painful, shameful struggle that placing a child for adoption was for me, I didn't believe I would ever have any more children. However, eight years later, I did.

When my daughter was six months old, my (placed) son had his ninth birthday. It was a tough day for me. Not only was I exhausted from sleep deprivation, mom life, and peer pressure, I was grieving all the things I didn't get to do and be there for with my son. I looked at my husband and said, "How am I ever going to tell her?"

My husband knew what I meant. How was I going to tell our daughter that I placed a child, her half-brother, for adoption? How was she going to feel that she didn't get to be a part of her life because of my choices? How was I going to answer her questions? No longer was I the only one in this story. He belonged to her as well. He was part of her story.

When I placed him for adoption, I didn't anticipate any of that. I made both an informed choice and an unavoidably ignorant decision. Would my daughter understand any of that? She was so tiny, so innocent, which is what I remember feeling about my son when I made that huge decision that changed both of our lives.

My husband, God love him, looked at me calmly and said, "You're going to practice. Go in there (to her room), and tell her right now." I felt a kind of stunned silence and a deep sense of peace. I took my daughter into her room and looked at her while I told her the whole story. I didn't hold back anything. When I was done, she was asleep, and I was relieved. It was no longer a secret between us, or a part of me I would hide from her. She knew everything, and I could practice telling her again when I needed to or when she needed to know more of the story.

As she grew, I did practice telling her, and she did need to know more about the story. Some of the conversations were hard.

No, Daddy isn't his daddy.
Yes, I do miss him.
No, your grandpa and granny, aunts and uncles don't talk about him ever.

Other conversations were easier.

He is a boy.
He likes soccer.
He is almost as tall as Daddy.

In the conversations, the one thing I lamented the most is that I didn't pursue more openness. I wish my daughter could ask him these questions herself. That is part of the vulnerability that goes along with parenting with a whole heart. I feel exposed and uncertain in the midst of the emotional risk when talking about placing my son for adoption with my daughter. I'm scared of what she will think of me. I'm worried she will decide I suck as a mom. I don't want her to question my love for her because it looks different from my love for him.

With my youngest son, the conversations about his older brother are less about his brother and more about his fear. I distinctly remember watching *Kung Fu Panda 2* with our family and my youngest son screaming and crying and running out of the room when the Mama Panda placed Po inside the basket in the river and watched him float away.

"I don't want you to do that to me," my youngest son sobbed. What could I say to him at that moment? 'I would never do that?' No, because I did do that to his older brother and he knew it. Instead, I wept with him, told him I was sorry that it scared him and did my best to assure him it was okay to feel scared or angry about it. He could always talk to me when he needed to about his brother's adoption.

Because I had other children, I no longer controlled the narrative in our community either. My children talk about their adopted brother, stunning children and adults with this information when they know another boy doesn't live in our house. It was a good thing I was comfortable in my skin as a birthmom and talking about adoption because as soon as my kids were old enough, I would get asked by any number of people openly doubtful or in hushed whispers about this adopted child. *Yes*, I would assure them, *he is real, and he is adopted.*

Through my three children, I have learned that adoption doesn't just have a triad. It's not just me, him and his parents. It's my kids as well and if applicable someday his kids too. This is not something you can hold close and never share. When there are other children involved, it gets bigger, messier somehow.

My children see me vulnerable and joyful and sad and relieved for a brother they do not live with. They speak of him and celebrate his birthday with me. He belongs to them as much as he does to me, and for as scary as it is to put myself out there with my own children, it's beautiful too because they know me on a deeper level than most of the people in my life.

My kids know their hearts can hurt and the sun can shine at the same time. They have seen grief and joy born out of the same moment. They are learning that belonging is a heart status and that they can love someone from far away and mean it.

In what ways have you/do you plan to talk to your children about adoption? How will/have you talk to them about being a birthmother? Who do you have to debrief with when you have hard conversations with your children? How can you honor their adopted sibling within your family? How can you foster an environment of love and belonging for a sibling who does not live with you? How can you involve your children in their sibling's life? Who are the key people in your child's life that might need to know about your child's adopted sibling? What books/movies/ people can you bring into your family/home that will spark conversation and help your children to understand adoption better?

BE YOU to full, *Beautiful!*

BE YOU to full, *Beautiful!*

BE YOU to full, *Beautiful!*

BE YOU to full, *Beautiful!*

BE YOU to full, *Beautiful!*

BE YOU to full, *Beautiful!*

BE YOU to full, *Beautiful!*

ONGOING HELP

As you know by now, this birthmom thing is lifelong and excruciating. It's not a walk in the park and no one will have all the answers. I know that while this book may be helpful, it is not an all-inclusive fix to anything. If you have worked through it and think, "Great. What's next?" I want to offer a list of resources for you.

First, reach out to your local birthparent support group, counselor, adoption agency, and/or pregnancy resource center. They may have some good contacts for you. I believe that face-to-face interactions can be the most helpful and healing for some people.

Books

Revealing You: A Journal for Birthmothers by Michelle Thorne
The Gifts of Imperfection by Brené Brown (anything by her really!)
Resolving Everyday Conflict by Ken Sande and Kevin Johnson
A Grace Disguised by Jerry Sittser (a good book on grief and loss)

Websites

www.adoption.com
www.birthmombuds.com
www.bravelove.org
www.brenebrown.com
www.lifetimehealingadoption.com
www.oyff.org
www.threestrandsinc.org

I also have learned a ton from adoptee and adoptive parent books and websites. These are hard to read sometimes but worth it. Remember, that conflict in your heart is an opportunity for connection.

REFERENCES

Brown, C. Brené. The Gifts of Imperfection: Let Go of Who You Think You're Supposed to Be and Embrace Who You Are. Hazelden, 2010.

Sande, Ken. Resolving Everyday Conflict. Baker Book House, 2015.

ACKNOWLEDGEMENTS

God. Thanks for loving me. I love You too.

Matthew. The cheerleader needed the artist as much as the artist needed the cheerleader. Who knew? I like me better when I'm with you.

My children. My teachers. My loves. My lights. My joys. You all are everything, everything.

Dan Simeone. Religion and poltics are okay, but heart conversations are best. I'm thankful I can call you anytime for one of those. I'm sorry we can relate over the deaths of our moms. Nancie with an IE and no K, whose name is not Susan, was a good one. Oh, and the website is stellar and much appreciated too.
www.gestaltcreations.com

Sallie Mosely. You are pure beauty. Your heart, face, life, worship, and photography being some of the ways I see it portrayed in you.
www.salliemoselyphotography.com

Becky Bruns & Beth James. I couldn't ask for better friends. Thank you for loving me as I am. I belong to you two and you both belong to me.

Holly Eskridge. You are my person. I can't believe I am lucky enough to know you and have you as a close friend. It's truly a priviledge. Thank you for believing in me and inspiring me with your confidence, strength, and a kind heart.

LaWanda Jones. Thanks for being a safe person and place for me to process and be myself in this crazy expat experience. I would not survive China without you. I love you dearly.

Kim Kizzia. I don't know why you put up with me, but I'm glad you do. Thank you for being a rock. I love you, friend.

CityChurch Charlotte. I'm still so grateful for the encouragement and space to be me and begin following God through writing way back in 2011. God continues using it.

Birthmoms. What can I say, girls? I love each of you. I am thankful I am not alone, and neither are you.

About the Author

Michelle Thorne is a believer in Jesus, vulnerability, inclusion, self-acceptance, and brokenness. She laughs loud and often and talks non-stop about adoption, shame and grief. When Michelle is being herself, she is usually taking in a work of art, reading a good book, enjoying a craft beer, or cheering for the Oklahoma Sooners, Carolina Panthers, New York Yankees, or Eintracht Frankfurt. Michelle lives with her husband and their two children in Qingdao, China.

www.michellethornebooks.com

Made in the USA
Monee, IL
15 December 2023

49435432R00129